Goldilocks and the three bears

by
Lucinda Pearce-Higgins

Illustrated by Maggie Read

Storyteller

Father Bear

Mother Bear

Baby Bear

Goldilocks

I don't like this porridge.
It is too salty.

Then she tasted the middle size bowl of porridge.

I don't like this porridge.
It is too sweet.

 Then she tasted the small bowl of porridge.

 This porridge is just right. Yum! Yum!

 And Goldilocks ate it all up.

Oh dear! I am tired.
I must sit down for a bit.

Then Goldilocks saw three chairs.
She saw a big chair for Father Bear
and she saw a middle size chair for
Mother Bear and she saw a small
chair for Baby Bear.

I think I will sit down over there.

 So Goldilocks sat down in the big chair.

 I don't like this chair.
It is too hard.

 Goldilocks sat down in the middle size chair.

 I don't like this chair.
It is too soft.

 So Goldilocks sat down in the small chair.

 This chair is just right.

 But just as Goldilocks sat down, there was a big **crack**!
She had broken the chair!

Oh dear! I am tired.
I want to go to sleep.

So Goldilocks went upstairs and she saw three beds.
There was a big bed for Father Bear and a middle size bed for Mother Bear and a little bed for Baby Bear.

I will just lie down for a little rest.

So Goldilocks lay down on the big bed.

I don't like this bed.
It is too long.

Then Goldilocks lay down on the middle size bed.

I don't like this bed.
It is too wide.

So Goldilocks lay down on the little bed.

This bed is just right.

And Goldilocks went fast asleep.

Once upon a time there were three bears.
They lived in a house in the woods.
One morning Mother Bear got up and went downstairs to the kitchen.
She made a big pot of porridge.

Wake up Father Bear.
It's time for breakfast.
Wake up Baby Bear.
It's time for breakfast.

Mother Bear put the porridge into three bowls.
There was a big bowl for Father Bear, a middle size bowl for Mother Bear and a small bowl for Baby Bear.

 My porridge smells good but it is too hot.

 My porridge smells good but it is too hot.

And my porridge smells good but it is too hot.
I can't eat it.

Let's all go for a walk in the woods
until the porridge gets cool.

So they shut the door and
went for a walk in the woods.
Just then Goldilocks came by and
saw the house of the three bears.

I wonder who lives in this house?
I'll go inside and have a look.

So Goldilocks pushed open the door
and went inside.
She looked at the kitchen table and
she saw the three bowls of porridge.

That porridge looks good.
I'll just taste some.

Goldilocks picked up a spoon and she tasted the big bowl of porridge.

Soon the three bears came back from their walk.

I am hungry.
I want my porridge.

I am very hungry.
I want my porridge.

I am very, very hungry.
I want my porridge and
I shall eat it all up.

 So they pushed open the door and went inside.
They looked at the kitchen table.

 Who's been eating my porridge?

 And who's been eating my porridge?

 And who's been eating my porridge?
They have eaten it all up!

 And Baby Bear began to cry.

Then Father Bear looked at his chair.

Who's been sitting in my chair?

And who's been sitting in my chair?

And who's been sitting in my chair?
Look! They have broken it all
to bits.

And Baby Bear cried even more.

 Let's go and look upstairs.

 So the three bears went upstairs.

 Who's been sleeping in my bed?

 And who's been sleeping in my bed?

 And who's been sleeping in my bed?
Look! There's someone still there!

The three bears looked at
the little bed.
They saw Goldilocks fast asleep.
Just then she opened her eyes and
looked at the three bears.
She saw Father Bear and
she saw Mother Bear and
she saw Baby Bear and
they were all looking at her!

Why are you sleeping in my bed?
And why have you broken my chair?
And why have you eaten
all my porridge?

What is your name?

And who are you?

Goldilocks jumped out of bed.

My name is Goldilocks.
I am very sorry Baby Bear.

But Baby Bear was so cross that he chased her downstairs.

 Goldilocks ran out of the house and into the wood.

 Never mind, Baby Bear.
I will make you some more porridge.

 And I will mend your chair.

 And I hope I will never see Goldilocks again.

 And he never did.